T0130476

The Adventures of Bosco

Written by
Paige Nicole Benningfield Dierker

Illustrated by Authorhouse

© 2006 Paige Nicole Benningfield Dierker. All rights reserved.

No part of this book may be reproduced, stored in a retrieval system, or
transmitted by any means without the written permission of the author.

AuthorHouse™
1663 Liberty Drive
Bloomington, IN 47403
www.authorhouse.com
Phone: 833-262-8899

Because of the dynamic nature of the Internet, any web addresses or links contained in this book may have changed
since publication and may no longer be valid. The views expressed in this work are solely those of the author and do not
necessarily reflect the views of the publisher, and the publisher hereby disclaims any responsibility for them.

This book is printed on acid-free paper.

ISBN: 978-1-4259-1907-8 (sc)
ISBN: 978-1-4678-5176-3 (e)

Print information available on the last page.

Published by AuthorHouse 02/22/2023

authorHOUSE®

WELCOME

I would like to dedicate this book to my wonderful family and friends. My mommy Paige is the author and of course my daddy Patrick and sister Gabrielle are a huge part of everything I did and still do. My Momo Jeanne and Papa Frank always had bones for me and played with me. They made sure I knew they loved me. They let me know they cared! Pappa Frank and I always had a lot of fun together! Abby my cousin played with me whenever she came over to our house and I liked her very much. Come to think of it...her mommy Aunt Tiffany and my Aunt Mary played with me too... Alex, one of my oldest cousins, thought I was cool and I thought he was cool...oh and all the other cousins were great. Papa Wayne could come into my home anytime and I would just stay right where I was... military mode on Gabrielle's bed doing my guard duty and not being disrupted! Anyone who knew me would know this was rare. I was on top of every single person who walked in the front door, including Grandma Dorothy, Wayne's wife. It was my duty of course! Gabrielle and her friend Madison were a big part of my younger years. The Adventures of Bosco will tell you more about this. I've been lucky - very lucky. Meadowbrook took great care of me too! I had a great family and I still do have a great family. I want you all to know that I'm watching from above! Patrick, Gabrielle and Mommy... I love you with all my heart and will never forget our hikes, long walks, and hugs.! So in short, this book is for you all!

Argh! Argh! Argh! Argh!
Bosco

"Urgh! Urgh! Urgh! Oh, excuse me. I forgot whom I was speaking to. English is better suited for you. Doggy Talk, which is my primary language, has always been hard for people to understand. So, I promise to speak to you on your level from here on out."

"My name is Bosco. I'd like to be able to tell you that my family had a very special reason for naming me Bosco, but unfortunately I can't. When my owners adopted me from the pet store, my name was really Roscoe. My mom, dad, and sister Gabrielle thought the pet store person called me Bosco. It really has never bothered me that my owners are hard of hearing. I have such incredible hearing that I can hear for all of us. Anyway, ever since the day I was adopted, I've had not only a new home but a new name as well. And you know what, it doesn't bother me one bit. Bosco fits me better than Roscoe ever did."

"I feel like the luckiest dog alive. I have two dog bowls. Both are china, decorated beautifully, and have 'King of the household' written on them. My collar is the coolest around. It's brown leather with gold X's and O's on it. I use to like to try and pop the little gold letters off so that I could chew on them. But then I met Muffy."

"My sister Gabrielle, who is eight years old, was going out the front door to play one day. I decided to follow her. It was such a beautiful day and the air was so sweet, the breeze so perfect, and my senses were soaring. By the time I stopped running, I couldn't see Gabrielle anywhere behind me. I wasn't worried though. She was a tough kid and took good care of herself. What I did see, however, was a vision of pure puppytopia! Muffy! Muffy! Muffy! Bow-Wow! Yes, Muffy was her name and she was my game. So, after a doggy moments thought, I decided to bring Muffy home with me. It wasn't too hard helping her get rid of her chain. I have really strong jaws and sharp teeth. I had her freed up in no time. My mom was really happy to see me, and Gabrielle ran to me and hugged me hard. I couldn't figure out why they were so happy, but I was so glad that they liked Muffy. Ever since then, I make sure that my X's and O's stay on my collar so that I look spiffy and neat for Muffy."

"Ever since I met Muffy, at least once a day I try and follow my sister Gabrielle out the front door, garage door, or back door. Adventure is in my blood and I just have to get out and visit all my new friends around the neighborhood. One day, I met a really big black longhaired dog, named Jake. He is probably my best buddy, besides Muffy that is. He's always fenced in his back yard so I run over to see him and we run the fence together. Jake runs it on the inside and I run it on the outside. Yesterday while I was making my rounds and had just finally made it over to Jakes, I saw a man pushing a very interesting cart. It had tall poles and buckets of fish in it. I had to check it out so I ran across the street and up to the man with all the neat stuff. He told me he was going fishing, showed me his bait, and asked me if I wanted to come. It sounded like fun and I was ready to go with him, when my mommy called out my name. She was running really fast today and smiling at the nice man who had invited me to go fishing. I really wanted to go with the nice man but Mommy looked like she wanted to spend some time with me. So I barked thank you and the man went on his way."

"I decided to take Mommy back over to Jake's house to play. I took off running again, over to Jake's of course, and mommy quickly followed. She ran up and down the fence with Jake and me: back and forth and back and forth. I decided since we were having so much fun that I should take Mommy over to my most special spot of all. I told Jake goodbye and ran back across the street, more slowly this time so Mommy could keep up. Mommy followed me through the trees, down the paths, and to the pond. We were having such a great time! The only things missing today were Gabrielle and her friend Madison. For some reason they'd gone home on their bikes a long time before. I think they had gotten tired of playing because mommy had soon replaced them."

"The pond was so peaceful today. The water moved just slightly and it looked so inviting. All of a sudden I was super hot and I had to cool down. I slowly made my way into the water and just sat in the same position for a few minutes. The water surrounded my entire body up to my neck. My panting became easier to control. Mommy was smiling at me and giggling. I just love my Mommy. The water felt so good that I decided to take a swim. Mommy threw me a few sticks and I retrieved them for her. It's what I do best being a Golden Retriever mixed breed of course. And after I had done my duty for my Mommy, fetching three sticks in a row, I decided to get dried off. I got out of the pond and shook the water out of my coat. I love doing that."

"Mommy moved away from me so she wouldn't get wet. I didn't blame her one bit. And when I was finished drying off, my nose took on a life of it's own. I could smell all the newly blooming flowers and bushes. I picked up the scents of all the different animals in the woods. The path back up to the road no longer looked interesting. I decided to take Mommy on a new adventure. I ran back up through the woods, over rocks, through bushes, around trees, sniffing everything as we hustled through the mud and leaves. Mommy was never too far behind."

"I decided to take Mommy through some of the neighbor's yards, whom I knew she hadn't met yet. Just as I reached the little puppy that was sunning itself on it's owner's patio, ready to do an appropriate greeting by sniffing noses, my Mommy grabbed me by my collar and told me it was time to go home."

"Mommy was very quiet the entire walk home. I sensed she was tired from our adventure. When we got inside our house, Gabrielle and Madison were eating their grilled cheese sandwiches Mommy had been making before I went on my outing. They looked at me kind of funny. I looked up at Mommy and I knew what Mommy's look meant.
Kennel Time!"

Paige Nicole Benningfield Dierker is the author of my story <u>The Adventures of Bosco</u>. She lives in the Midwest with her husband, my daddy, Patrick and Gabrielle my sister, her daughter. My family now has a new puppy named Pogie Po, who I very much approve of for them. I continue to live in the hearts of all who loved me, so my mommy says, and she says they all still do love me very much! I now reside in Heaven and as my mommy Paige says, I have a very important job! I run errands upstairs for the big guy himself... yes the number one numero uno God! So, if you ever see my best friend Jake running the fence like he's having fun, just know that I'm right there with him. I'd be taking my break at that point. I'm no slacker! I'm Bosco from <u>The Adventures of Bosco</u>!

Future Books to Look for from Paige:

The Adventures of Bosco 2

Pogie Po Goes Chic

The Tales of Granny Applesweet

Quotes for a New Millennium

Printed in the United States
by Baker & Taylor Publisher Services